MOONROCKET

THE THRILLER RIDE OF THE THIRTIES

THE FAIRGROUND ASSOCIATION OF GREAT BRITAIN · 1988

Above: An early Heyn Moonrocket, Belgian showman Ant. Benner's 'O Boot Flotille'. (A. Lefebvre)

Title page: The two Moonrocket centre figures on display at Wookey Hole Caves, the curious 'Man with Scarf' and Popeye, both by Lakin's.

Acknowledgements

This booklet has been compiled over a number of years from information supplied by many people to whom we wish to express our thanks. Particular thanks must go to Jack Leeson, whose earlier notes on these machines proved the largest single source of information; and to Philip Bradley and Rowland Scott who, as well as providing much information, also supplied many of the photographs. Special thanks also go to Michael Bonhoff who provided the information on the origins and the development of the machine in Germany.

Kevin Scrivens
Stephen Smith

MOONROCKET
THE THRILLER RIDE OF THE THIRTIES

General History

The Moonrocket, which became known in Britain through the magnificent Lakin/Maxwell machines of the late 1930s, was actually invented and developed in Germany.

It is believed that the first machine to bear any resemblance to the Moonrocket was a modified switchback-type ride, introduced in the late 1920s or early '30s by Friedrich Heyn of Neustadt/Orla, a well known German ride builder and carver.

This ride was open topped, with a low front and high back, and had a counter-rotating centre. It differed from later machines in that it had a shallow dip at each side of the high rear hill.

The first machines are thought to have been boat rides, with eight large boat cars and a lighthouse in the centre. Later machines still incorporating the rear dips had sixteen "bob" cars, and a Snowman in the centre.

In 1936 Friedrich Heyn introduced the "Schragbahn", the slanting rail circle with no dips. The platforms were fitted with two segmented rocket tubes of metal-cased plywood, and the ride was known as the "Rocket Ride to the Moon". The centre dome, or globe as it was known in Germany, was fitted with two small rockets; one carrying a small child and the other a man with long hair, derived, it is thought, from a German nursery story about a boy who takes a trip to the moon.

All the Moonrockets that left the Neustadt workshops were open topped. Some showmen experimented with tunnels at the back of the ride, but the idea was quickly abandoned due to the suction caused by the rocket tubes passing through the tunnel. Some machines did have custom built roofs later fitted to protect them from the weather. At least one such machine still travels.

In November 1936, German showman Carl Bohm presented the first Moonrocket to appear at Hamburg Dom Fair. This fair was visited by Messrs Hoadley, Maxwell, and Lakin, on a trip from Britain looking for new ideas. Bohm's Moonrocket obviously impressed John Hoadley, and on his return to Britain he put in an order for a similar machine to be built by Maxwell/Lakin - the former to produce the mechanical parts, and Lakins to complete and decorate; an arrangement that was already in existence between the two firms in building machines such as Arks and Mont Blancs. The British machine made its debut at Hull Fair in 1937.

Heyn's factory was one of the victims of the Second World War, at the end of which Neustadt found itself in the eastern part of divided Germany. This virtually ended German Moonrocket manufacture.

In West Germany the heavy blitz destroyed much showmen's equipment, but several of the original Moonrockets survived. Some of these are still travelling, although with the advent of modern space theme rides, these have reverted to the earlier winter sports themes.

Several Heyn machines were exported, one of which came to Britain. Of those that went to America, one was discovered packed away in the late '70s. It was refurbished, and taken on the road once more.

An unknown French manufacturer built at least one Moonrocket, but apart from the photograph of the machine, nothing is known about it.

German survivor from pre-war days, Vespermann's Rocket at Rendsberg, 1977. (M. Bonhoff)

The only known French Moonrocket, Degruson's 'La Fusee'. (A. Lefebvre)

In Britain

On 11th December 1936, Chas. Openshaw of Reading applied for a patent relating to virtually an exact copy of the Heyn machines, even down to the rocket cars. The complete specification was left at the Patent Office on 27th October 1937 (by which time Hoadley's machine was built and operating) and was accepted on 22nd March 1938.

The patent drawing was a copy of the Heyn machines, having the same stays in the gates. These were different on the Maxwell machines.

It is not known how or why Chas. Openshaw was able to patent a machine that was not his idea, and which had been built and was operating in both Germany and Britain over a year before the patent was accepted.

Maxwell/Lakin built at least fourteen machines, all extremely similar in construction and appearance. The bottoms of the machines were very much like their German counterparts. The rear gates were very high, and consequently heavy, and there were also many stays to keep the ride stable. The rear shutters were so deep that they were made in three sections, a small lower one and two hinged upper ones.

The British manufacturers decided that our inclement weather made a roof essential, a feature which added to the cumbersome construction. Due to the revolving centre, there was no static central support for the rafters. To overcome this, two heavy Dodgem-type principals were bolted together to bridge the machine from reinforced uprights at each side. This unit was supported by a third principal from the centre to the front of the machine. From this solid arrangement normal rafters and stays were fitted.

They were on average 52 feet in diameter, actually an ellipse in plan. The four-wheel centre was most common, it had a 25 h.p. main drive motor, which drove the cheese wheel, and a 5 h.p. motor which drove the centre cone. In some instances the front lock of the centre truck was removed to build up the machine, in others small pits were dug to take the front wheels.

The cheese wheel held twenty swifts, four of which were stayed, and these carried twenty platforms. The rocket tubes were formed in sections, one on each platform, seating four people in two compartments. Two opposite platforms were empty, leaving space for the front and rear overhang of the two rockets. The seating capacity was 72. The centre cone held twenty smaller swifts which carried the dome sections.

The cars revolved clockwise at about 12 r.p.m., while the centre dome revolved anti-clockwise at 6 r.p.m., creating an illusionary speed of 18 r.p.m. This is surprisingly fast in a comparatively small circle at

almost ground level.

The decoration was fairly standard, although there appears to have been two distinct types of front boards. One, in a comic strip vein, had cloud-shaped tops to the boards; the other type had smooth, curved-topped boards.

On the centre dome of each of the Lakin machines was a small wooden rocket, usually carrying a figure of Popeye. This led to the machine becoming known as "The Popeye" in some areas. When John Hoadley's machine was new it had a figure of an old man, his scarf blowing behind him. William Codona's machine had a similar figure, and one of these is now on show at Wookey Hole Caves. Albert Holland's had a second small rocket opposite Popeye with a figure of Olive Oyl riding it.

Orton & Spooner, surprisingly, built only one Moonrocket. An open-topped machine, it looked very similar to its German counterparts.

The last known Moonrocket type ride to have been built was as late as 1965, by the German manufacturers Mack of Waldkirch. The bottom is much the same as the earlier machines, but the cars are twenty, two-seater boats. The uprights are in the shape of palm trees, and support a roof with an open centre section.

On 7/1/53 W. Codona was granted a patent, number 717695, which related to the modification of a Moonrocket. This involved fitting a number of smaller

Studies in geometry: Above, the centre of Walter Shaw's machine, showing the swifts and stays. Also visible are the slots for the dome swifts at the base of the cone. Below, the complex roof structure of the same ride. Burnley, 14.7.81. (K.T. Scrivens)

cars on the platforms, each free to swing independently by centrifugal force, or by the exertions of the patrons. In both conversions made in Britain, the number of platforms was reduced to sixteen, and each of these was fitted with a rocket shaped car.

At least one similar conversion was made in Germany, but in that case the cars were boat shaped, with facing seats. It is not known if this conversion was made before or after 1953.

Above: Joe Ling's Leyland Hippo and box truck, with the roof principals fastened to their sides, on the Pond Street site, Sheffield, 17.7.45. (P.W. Bradley)

Below: Ling's Moonrocket centre truck on the Forest Recreation Ground, Nottingham , prior to the build-up of the Goose Fair, 1.10.62. (P.W. Bradley)

Transport

The Moonrocket centres were notable for being the first type of machine centres to come out of Maxwells on pneumatics. Transport arrangements no doubt differed, but usually the machines came with two Maxwell box trucks, and two four-wheel flat trucks. One of the box trucks was higher and shorter than the other. This was used for storing the cars in an upright position, and some, if not all the shutters. The other box truck carried the front boards, roundings, handrails, steps, gag cards, dome sections and, if necessary, the remainder of the shutters. One box truck would carry the two main principals, one on each side, and the other box the front principal. Uprights were carried on top of the box trucks, and quarterings and swifts fitted in the cells beneath the box bodies. The two flat trucks carried the bottom of the machine, i.e. sleepers, gates, stays, etc.

In several instance the two four-wheel trucks were replaced by a six-wheel truck which carried most of the bottom, and it was not uncommon to see the trams carried on the centre truck, along with some of the gratings.

Initially, many of the British machines were hauled by showmen's steam traction engines, which of course generated for the machines when they were built up and open. One example is Joe White's machine which travelled with their 65 b.h.p. Foster 13075 "Teddy", and it is interesting to quote the late Bill Oswald's recollection of this in the N.T.E.C. publication "Steaming" Vol 12 No 1. 'This was the biggest of White's engines and she was attached to the Moonrocket, a rather heavy machine. The power output needed to drive it was evident when one watched "Teddy" on the belt, at times she seemed to make rather heavy work of it, and the exhaust sounded fierce.'

However, soon after the introduction of the Moonrocket, showmen's engines went into a decline, and after the war diesel transport took over. At first tractors were used as prime movers, but even they were soon discarded in favour of lorry loading: box bodied lorries replaced the box trucks, flat bed lorries replaced the flat trucks. When the last Moonrocket to travel, Walter Shaw's, ceased operations its transport arrangements comprised the original low Maxwell box, a newer high box, and an eight-wheel Atkinson which carried the bottom of the machine.

The most unusual transport arrangement was that used by Michael A. Collins, who at one time employed two Foden steam wagons with his machine.

Moonrockets Operated In Britain

Heyn

John Collins

The first Moonrocket to operate in Britain. It was imported by the firm of Schippers, and delivered to Norwich Easter Fair, 1937. During 1941 it spent some time at New Brighton and was advertised for sale. It was a standard Heyn open-top machine, but by Birmingham Onion Fair, 1949, a top had been fitted. There are no details of how the roof was supported, but it was said to be unlike the Lakin tops. The tops of the front and roundings were all the same level, the roundings only reaching half-way to the back of the ride. The bottom edge, however, dipped towards the front sections forming a deeper front.

It was later purchased by Albert Barton, and rebuilt in Hereford. It operated at Barry Island for two seasons in partnership with Bernard Saunt and was then sold to Webber Bros of Rhyl, who operated it at the amusement park there for two or three seasons, following which it was thought to have been scrapped.

This machine appeared at many fairs under the Pat Collins' banner, and has been recorded as a separate machine, belonging to Pat Collins. However, there is no evidence that there were two machines.

Blackpool Pleasure Beach

Another Heyn Moonrocket operated at Blackpool's famous Pleasure Beach during the Second World War. A film made there shows that the counter-rotating centre carried a rocket with two strange figures riding it. The rear scenery was also unusual in that the twelve boards carried paintings of the signs of the Zodiac. Like the John Collins' machine it was open topped.

A German showman, Joachim Drescher, bought a German Moonrocket from a British amusement park, which had been in this country about twenty five years. Whilst in Britain the rear of the machine had stalls set in under the gratings, which suggests the machine is possibly the one which operated at the Pleasure Beach.

Since its return to its country of origin it has undergone more changes, the most notable being the fitting of a level, i.e. not sloping roof, which is of necessity extremely high at the front. The roof structure came from a scrapped German Mont Blanc, and has the characteristic dome shape of that type of machine. It now has twenty small two-seater rocket cars.

Above: Ex Blackpool Pleasure Beach? Joachim Drescher's 'Apollo 11', Poppenbuttel, May 1979. (M. Bonhoff)

Below: John Collins' Heyn Moonrocket at Great Yarmouth, August, 1948. (J.R. Scott)

John W Hoadley
This, the first machine built in Britain, made its debut at Hull Fair in 1937. It originally travelled with Burrell 3072 "Daisy", which was replaced by a Scammell tractor that was dwarfed by the machine. It travelled in the north-east of England, and made an annual visit to Hull Fair. In 1949 it spent the season at the Spanish City amusement park at Whitley Bay, but came out at the end of the year for Hull Fair.

On 11/12/49 it was sold to J.W.Leonard, and was delivered and built up in the Kelvin Hall, Glasgow, by Hoadleys. In June 1950, after being advertised for sale, it was bought by Blackpool Pleasure Beach, where it spent only a short while before being sold to Helters of Southport for the amusement park there. By 1955 it was looking rather sad with no decoration. It was eventually acquired by J & H Shaw, who used the centre and some of the bottom for their 1958 Maxwell Waltzer. The Waltzer is now owned by Gary Gore. The centre remains immediately recognisable as a former Moonrocket centre and is in remarkable condition.

It is thought that an attempt was made to use the main principals from this machine on Walter Shaw's Moonrocket, but it was found that they were too short. This tends to confirm the view that the machines were individually constructed, starting at the bottom and being made to fit as they were built up, rather than being assembled from pre-constructed parts.

William Codona
Delivered new to Galston in April 1938, and travelled Scotland until 1947 when it was sold to Aquilla Toogood. It then travelled the north-east, attending Newcastle Town Moor each year until 1954. It spent the 1955 season in Battersea Park, and was then taken to South Africa by the manager, Tucker Caris.

Above: J.W. Hoadley's Moonrocket, Hull, 16.10.48. (J.R. Scott)
Left: William Codona's ride at Bellahouston, 21.7.41. (W. Cross)
Below: Helter's machine at Southport in July, 1955. (J.R. Scott)

Michael A Collins

New for Gorton Wakes Fair in September 1938, it was one of the few machines to have had a two-wheel centre. As previously mentioned, it had the unusual transport arrangement of two Foden steam wagons, one of which had a Fowler diesel generating set fitted to its chassis.

The machine was open at Gorton Wakes one year later when war was declared. Together with Collins's other machines it was hastily pulled down and taken to Queens Road, Harpurhey, where it remained packed up for some time.

The machine opened at a few fairs in 1940, accompanied by the Burrell 3291 "Emperor", but during that year it was sold, and M.A. Collins's Dragons, a more popular ride, was returned to the road in its place.

Its new owner was F. Thompson who operated it at Belle Vue, Manchester in 1941-42. It was then sold to E. Brennan who operated it at New Brighton until the early 1960s.

Sarah Anne Proctor

New at South Normanton Feast, September 1938, and appeared at Wanstead Flats at Easter 1939, still without front boards. At this time it carried the name "The Rocket" in cut-out letters across the front. On the road it was accompanied by two Armstrong Saurers, which were lettered "The Strato Rocket", a name later used for the swing-out car machines of which this was to be the first, albeit fourteen years later.

During the war it was sold to E.L. Morley, and was travelled around Lancashire and Cheshire. It visited the wartime Goose Fairs at Nottingham, which were then held at Whitsun. In 1945 the ride's front was re-shaped and redecorated, and the cars were re-upholstered. In this, as new condition, it was advertised for sale on 21/6/45 while it was open on Stalybridge market place.

It was sold to J.W. Leonard of Scotland who advertised it for sale on 18/8/45, claiming that ill health forced the sale.

It was sold to John Codona and travelled Scotland for two years before being sold to Hibble & Mellors in 1947. In their ownership it travelled the Notts and Derby area, visiting the Goose Fair each year. It even made at least one foray into Lancashire in 1948, still carrying John Codona's name. By 1952 it had been sold to H.S. Gray of the Eastern Counties, but at the end of that year had been sold once again, back into the Codona family, to William Codona.

Over the winter of 1952-3 it was converted to swing-out cars under the owner's own patent, and was redecorated as the "Stratorockets".

In this first conversion the individual rocket cars were rather angular, and wooden looking. Once again it travelled Scotland. In 1953 it made the long trek, together

Facing page, top: Originally made for Michael Albert Collins, the Moonrocket operated by E. Brennan at New Brighton, 22.10.52. (J.R. Scott)

Facing page, bottom: Early days in the life of the most-travelled Moonrocket of them all, Mrs S.A. Proctor's ride at Wanstead Flats, Easter 1939 – still awaiting its top boards. (P.W. Bradley)

This page, left: Nine years later, still bearing its previous (and fourth) owner's name, the much-travelled Moonrocket appears under the Hibble & Mellors banner on the Tommyfield, Oldham, 19.6.48. (J.R. Scott)

This page, above: Converted to swing-out cars and with a brand-new name, Mrs Mary Codona's Stratorockets decked out in flags and flowers for Queen Elizabeth the Second's Coronation, Woolwich Common, 30.5.53. (P.W. Bradley)

with other Scottish machines, down to Woolwich Common for the Coronation Fair held there in May. At this time it was in the hands of Mrs Mary Codona.

In July 1955 it was sold to Webber Bros of Rhyl, and operated at their amusement park for five years, retaining Codona's name on the decoration. This turned out to be fortunate, for in 1959 it was sold to Gordon Codona, and was thus returned to Scotland. By then it should have known its own way around!

In 1962 it was sold to Billy Manning, and was used at his Clarence Pier amusement park at Southsea. While here it was painted predominantly white. In 1967 it was sold to A. Stokes, but by 1968 was advertised for sale again, minus the top and centre dome.

Alas, no bid was forthcoming from any member of the Codona family, and it was broken up in 1968-9. This was the most sold, most travelled, and most altered Moonrocket in Britain.

Charles Heal

New for Cheltenham Easter Fair 1939. It took the place of the Four-abreast on much of their run, although the two machines did open together occasionally. The centre dome was not noted to have spun after 1945.

It last opened as Heal's in 1962, following which it was sold to W. Summers, and operated at Barry Island until 1968. At that time it was advertised for sale for £2000, with transport. It was said to be in reasonable condition, and had a good tilt but no balloon, which is odd as it opened as an open-top machine at Barry.

It was purchased by E. Silcock Jnr, but never opened by him. It is thought to have been used as a basis for the Silcock's Waltzer at Southport, but the centre on that looks nothing like that of a Moonrocket.

Part of the machine still travels: the four centre front boards were sold to Harry Hamer and form the front of his Orton Ark. Only the shape gives them away.

Joe White

New at Saltcoats May 1938, and travelled Scotland until 1949. This is the only Moonrocket known to have suffered (rather than caused) a fatality. It appears that a young man riding on the machine, being much the worse for drink, attempted to grab the Popeye as it passed him, resulting in his death. Because of this, Whites decided to part with the machine.

The ride appeared at the Kelvin Hall over Christmas and the New year, 1948-49, after which, in February 1949, it was sold to Rowlands of Cornwall. By the following July it was once again for sale, eventually being exchanged for Reuben Gillham's Lakin Ben-Hur. Gillham's travelled the Moonrocket on their South Coast run of fairs until 1951, when it was sold.

Above: Joe White's Moonrocket at Kirkcaldy Links Market, April 1939. (Stuart P. Johnstone) Below: Heal's Moonrocket with the Foden 'Blaise Castle' in attendance, Mitcham Common, 15.4.60. (P.W. Bradley)

Edward Danter

The only Moonrocket to travel South Wales. It was new for Pontypool Christmas Fair in 1938, and spent the 1939 season at Porthcawl Amusement Park, following Pontypridd Easter Fair. While in Danter's ownership it was featured in a G.P.O. promotional film. It is thought to have had a two-wheel centre, the same as M.A. Collins' machine.

In 1943 it was sold to the Belle Vue Amusement Co. and operated at their park in Manchester, replacing the John Collins ride.

In 1959 it was sold to Fred Thompson, and put on a permanent site at Mablethorpe. It is thought to have later passed to Silcock Bros, but was never travelled by them. It is not known why they bought it, but the purchase was to some extent confirmed by the fact that they were advertising a set of Moonrocket cars for sale in January 1960.

John Farrar

New for Doncaster St Leger Race Fair in September 1938. When it appeared at Lynn Mart the following year it was still without front or roundings, but these were delivered during that year.

It was advertised for sale on 4/8/45, but remained in Farrar's ownership until at least November 1946. It was sold to an operator at the Kursaal amusement park, Southend, in early 1947.

It was purchased in the early '50s by John Ling, and the centre and other parts were used in his 1953 Maxwell Waltzer. The Waltzer is now owned by Albert Evans, and the centre is still easily recognisable as being out of a Moonrocket.

Top: John Farrar's Moonrocket, Kings Lynn Mart, 1939. (Jewson's)

Left: Edward Danter's Moonrocket, Coney Beach, Porthcawl, 25.8.39. (P.W. Bradley)

Below: The same machine at Belle Vue, Manchester, in 1943.

Albert Holland

New Easter 1939, this machine attended only 10 fairs before the outbreak of war in September of that year. After storage during the war years it was travelled regularly throughout the east Midlands, its itinerary occasionally including the Goose Fair.

It was returned to Lakins in 1951 in part exchange for a new Dodgem track, later being exported by Lakins to South Africa.

Arthur Holland

New in early 1939, the roundings being delivered at Lincoln April Fair that year. The original front featured Snow White and the Seven Dwarfs in the rocket, pursued by a witch on a broomstick. This decoration was replaced in the late '40s or early '50s while in Holland's ownership with an unusual scene which can be seen in the photograph.

It passed to Bert Holland on his father's death, and last appeared in his ownership at Loughborough in 1956, following which it was replaced by a new Maxwell Waltzer. It was advertised for sale in the 'World's Fair' in 1957, and was sold to Butlins. It was used initially at their Clacton camp, but was later moved to Skegness, where it was last seen in 1966.

Top: An unusual view of Albert Holland's Moonrocket on Rugby Cattle Market in March, 1950, clearly showing the height of the three-section rear shutters and the imaginative lunar landscape decor. (J.R. Leeson)

Right: Arthur Holland's Moonrocket at Coventry Great Fair in May, 1951. The unconventional rocket on the then recently redecorated front boards was based, presumably, on the various experimental jet 'planes which were built in the immediate post-war years. (J.R. Leeson)

J.H. Shaw

Delivered new to Seaforth Easter Fair, Liverpool, but spent the summer at a south coast resort. During the war, son Walter was invalided out of the army and the machine passed to him. It travelled mainly in Lancashire, but was also seen quite frequently in Yorkshire.

In 1954 it was converted to a swing-out car machine by Maxwells under Codona's patent, fitted with a front canopy and false pillars and redecorated as "The Space Cruisers".

It was still travelling extensively until the late 1970s, but after that it began to make only rare appearances at the larger fairs, such as Newcastle, Nottingham, and Hull. One year it made the long journey up to Kirkcaldy.

The sixteen rocket cars fitted when the machine was converted were much more pleasing to the eye than those on the Codona machine, retaining the tube shape of the original long rocket cars.

In 1984 it was sold to Philip Knightsbridge, but has remained packed away since.

Top: Walter Shaw's Moonrocket in its original form at Hull Fair, 14.10.47. Among the passengers on the front boards would appear to be Popeye, Groucho Marx and Oliver Hardy. (J.R. Scott)

Left: 12 years later, and now bearing the name 'Space Cruisers', Shaw's machine boasts a set of swing-out cars, a front canopy, false pillars and new decor. Newcastle Town Moor Fair 20.6.59. (J.R. Scott)

Joe Ling

New in April 1938. This was the only machine not to have had the Earth and Moon at each side of the front boards when new, although the rest of the decoration was as on the other machines. It was based in Yorkshire but travelled extensively, appearing at places as far apart as London and Newcastle.

During the 1950s one of the flat trucks and its load were destroyed by fire. A new set of gates was made by a Lincolnshire joiner to replace those damaged in the fire, and the machine continued to travel until 1962.

The loads were taken to the yard at Burn, near Selby, and remained there for sixteen years, during which time they became very overgrown.

In 1978 the machine was purchased by Philip Knightsbridge, who intended to restore the machine to operating conditions.

Right: Yet another pre-war Easter visitor to Epping Forest minus its 'bonnet' – Joe Ling's Moonrocket, Wanstead Flats, 8.4.39. (P.W. Bradley)

Below: The artistic and comic genius of Edwin Hall, Lakin's chief decorator, is seen to advantage in this splendid shot taken on Ealing Common, 26.5.47. The figure leaning out of the painted rocket, looking decidedly travel-sick, bears an uncanny resemblance to Adolf Hitler! (P.W. Bradley)

Above: Billy Butlin's Moonrocket, Pond Street, Sheffield, August, 1944. Below: Billy Manning's Rocket at the Festival Pleasure Gardens, Battersea Park, 11.10.52. (P.W. Bradley)

Billy Butlin (1)
New 1938 for Clarence Pier, Southsea, which at that time was operated by Butlins.

Billy Butlin (2)
New 1939, probably for another of Butlin's permanent parks.

It is virtually impossible to distinguish between these two machines after they were new. Both left their seaside homes after 1940 to travel for the 'Holiday at Home' fairs, and one was recorded as far north as Huddersfield and Sheffield in 1944. After the war they were sighted at the Holiday Camps; one was reported at Littlehampton in 1948.

In 1949 Butlin's opened a Moonrocket at Olympia, London; so extensively had it been rebuilt that it appeared like a new machine. New rounding boards and front had been fitted, the shutters redecorated, and the cars, unlike those of pre-war days, had no doors.

In the early 1950s Billy Manning travelled this machine, although it spent at least the 1952 and 1953 seasons at Battersea Park. It eventually went to Clarence Pier, which Manning had acquired from Butlin's, and remained there until 1962 when it was replaced by the ex-Codona Stratorockets. Since then no trace can be found of it.

In the late 1950s Butlin's advertised one Moonrocket for sale from their Pwhelli camp, but by this time they had also acquired the ex-Arthur Holland machine. The final mention which has been found of either of these machines is in an advertisement in the 'World's Fair' in 1969, when two Rockets were advertised for sale, at Ayr and Filey. A late photograph of the machine at Filey shows that by then it was very plain. Not only was it open-topped, but the uprights had been cut-off at handrail level.

Hill Bros

As already stated, this was the sole example of an Orton-built Moonrocket. It was at Wormwood Scrubs at Easter, 1939, and was probably new not long before that. In 1940 it was sold to a showman in Ireland.

A Moonrocket was advertised for sale at the Belle Vue Amusement Park, Belfast, in May 1948, following the expiry of the park's lease. Advertised under the name of L. Levey, the machine was still there the year after, when it was described as being in 'rough condition' and not having been operated for some time. In the 'World's Fair' of 11/6/49 it was reported that the ride had been exported by W.H. Wilkie (of New Brighton) to Reykjavik, Iceland. Could this have been the Hill Bros machine?

Mystery Machines

Our research has left us with several mysteries. So far, a lack of fuller information has prevented us compiling more detailed histories of the following machines. For all we know, there may well be connections between these rides and those already described.

J.W. Leonard In 1946 Joe Leonard advertised for sale a Moonrocket which had been new to Southend Amusement Park in 1938.

Ramsgate Amusement Park A Moonrocket was advertised for sale from Ramsgate in October, 1949.

R. Grandison Advertised for sale in 1949.

Alf Harker This machine was reported at a number of fairs in the north-east of England, 1948-49. Believed to have been sold to Roy Carter, who travelled it with an unnamed partner. When this partnership broke up during the 1950s the ride was put up for sale by auction. No mention of its subsequent history has been found.

Fred Thompson Operated at Cleethorpes during the early 1950s. In 1954 it was advertised for sale from Hope Bank, Honley, at a price of £500. It was purchased by Alf Scott who used the centre in his Maxwell Waltzer. This machine is now travelled by Charles Jameson, still with its easily-distinguished Moonrocket centre truck.

J. Crole Advertised for sale from Porthcawl in November, 1957.

Myers Amusements (Isle of Man) Broken up for spares in 1968, the parts being advertised for sale.

Above: Hill Bros' Orton & Spooner Moon Rocket at Wormwood Scrubs, 7.4.39. (P.W. Bradley)

Right: Orton & Spooner works photographs of the front and rear cars from the two rocket tubes on the Hill Bros' machine.